THE BOOK OF
INTERFERING
BODIES

DANIEL
BORZUTZKY

THE BOOK OF
INTERFERING BODIES

NIGHTBOAT BOOKS

CALLICOON, NEW YORK

CONTENTS

*It is therefore crucial to find a way of routinizing,
even bureaucratizing, the exercise of imagination.*

– THE 9/11 COMMISSION REPORT

RESUSCITATION

I

I fell

I tripped over the horse corpse and its dead bones cracked

I was stuck between the horse legs and they came with a cleaver

Chop off the legs, they demanded

I chopped off the horse legs and the vermin that sucked on the dead beast
scrambled across the floorboards

I chopped the horse legs into thousands of pieces and they said what do
you see

I said I see thousands of bone shards and blood and bits of hair and in
each fragment there are villages, towns, hamlets, inlets, streets, suburbs,
cities, states, and countries

Nations or countries? They asked

Countries

They took the cleaver and sat me on the splattered horse legs and my body
was covered in blood

They brought me stale bread and as I ate they said make something for us, a
work of art, with the horse legs

Hundreds and thousands of leg bits and in each one a city a state a country
and I made the biggest tower they had ever seen and when it was
complete they said: destroy it

I ran into the tower and horse bones flew everywhere

They fired thousands of bullets into the horse legs

They struck a match and asked me if I wanted to burn with the horse legs

I said yes I would like to burn with the horse legs but they said tough shit
    and pulled me into the field by my hair
They ripped off my shirt and threw it into the flames
Find yourself another shirt, they said
Steal another shirt from one of the boys and don't let them say you can't
    have it
They fired a bullet near my feet and I ran towards the dormitories
The boys were sleeping
I found my friend on one of the bunks and asked him for his shirt
He gave me his shirt and wrapped himself in a moth-eaten blanket and I
    wanted to crawl in his bed to keep him warm
He gave me his shirt and we both knew he would freeze and when I went
    outside they said you shit how dare you take the shirt from a dying boy
    and they beat me and called me a heartless coward
They ripped the shirt off my back and they said steal yourself another shirt
The sun on the snow and shadows merged into doors and rooms
Crawl inside the doors and rooms, they said
I crawled into the snow and stayed there until they grew bored of watching
    me freeze

I I

They brought me to the tunnel

You watched me go inside

I saw your sketches on the walls of the tunnel:

A house, a small child playing, a tree, a dog, a ball of sunlight over a field of
   flowers

Erase, they said

They threw buckets and rags and bottles of bleach at me and said don't
   drink the bleach you worm

They sealed up the tunnel and disappeared and now I was in the dark and I
   could barely see the outlines of your sketches

Erase all memory of her life, they said

I scrubbed the wall of your drawings and I scrubbed you away

I scrubbed the wall and I imagined I created you as I destroyed your drawings

Your legs appeared on the wall and I pulled them off and I did the same
   with your arms and chest and face and mouth and hair

I stood you next to me and side by side we scrubbed the wall to destroy
   what little trace was left of you

They cracked the tunnel door and for a second I saw sunlight

They opened a cage of mice and released them into the tunnel

They threw bread at us

I scrambled for the bread but when they sealed up the tunnel it disappeared
   in the darkness

I listened to the sound of the mice chewing on the bread

I touched your head and it became a balloon

The warmth of my hand made your head swell with air and when your head
   exploded I found a rag and a bottle of bleach

I took a sip of the bleach and it was vinegar

I spit out the vinegar and watched your eyeballs sail down a river

I scooped up your eyeballs and tried to pin them to my chest

Your eyeballs dissolved into the cotton of my shirt and I imagined you
    could see inside of me

I felt your eyes inside of my chest and what they saw was an endless drip

Your eyes said follow the drip so I crawled through the mice to the other
    side of the tunnel where I heard water dripping from the ceiling

I stood beneath the drip and let the water fall into my hand

The water hit my hand one drop after another

I cupped the water in my hand and brought it to my mouth

I tasted you and you tasted like mildew and the drops went from my mouth
    to your lips and it was good to know I could nourish you and feel your
    mouth in my belly and hear you breathe as the mice ate through my
    pants and into the hair on my legs

It was good to feel your mouth in my belly as the mice crawled on my face
    and head

I knelt on the ground and prayed they would unseal the tunnel

You said they will never unseal the tunnel and you will rot here and I will
    love you

I felt your presence melt over me and together we refused to think

I carried your mouth inside of me as I lay down and refused to think

I I I

I followed your voice

You said go to the river and when I went to the river there was no voice and
I looked for you

I looked for your voice in the sand and all I found was a soldier's jacket
hanging from a branch

I looked in the pocket and there was a stack of passports and I looked for you

A voice found me looking through the passports and when he said drop it I
dove into the river

The water was freezing and as I dove in I heard a gun shot and I sank to the
bottom

I found your voice on the floor and I held it between my frozen fingers

I took your voice in my hand and prayed for it to give me warmth

I rubbed your voice against my chest and you said go back go back don't
leave go back don't leave

I pushed to the surface and my lungs would not open

The soldier held out a stick to me

He pulled me to the water and when I caught my breath he beat me with the stick

I told the soldier I had lost your body

He told me there were thousands of lost bodies and none of them would
ever find themselves

He said was the body blessed into heaven and I said there was no one to
bless it to heaven

He said I'm not a ghost though I look like one and he beat me with the
stick until I was unconscious

I woke up frozen without a passport but I found your voice

You said it is better to freeze than to melt but I did not believe you

You said let my voice drip over you and the heat will return to your body

Days passed

You disappeared as I waited for the heat and when you came back you were a rat and you opened your mouth and said come in me

I held open your mouth and looked into your body

I put my hand in your mouth and when you snapped at it I lay down and let my mouth fill with foam

I said have you seen my mother and father and you opened your mouth and there they were

I jumped in your rat body to be with my parents and we spoke of the good old days

You spoke of the good old days and your words were rain falls that washed my parents away

The rain means nothing here   your voice said

The rain means nothing here and your voice was a machine that made my parents disappear

You turned on the machine and typed in the code and when my mother and father disappeared there was only the sound of rain in your rat body

I let the rain pour over my head and I wondered who I would be when I came out of your voice

I felt for the pouch in my pants where I keep my passport

The soldier had taken my pants and all I had left was skin

I wanted to peel off my skin and dissolve into the tiniest voice

I started to peel the skin off my arms and worked my way up to my shoulder across my neck to the other shoulder along the arms down to the hand

I peeled the skin off my chest and stomach and in my rib cage your voice said peel more

I peeled off my skin wishing to be what I would never become and you said forget and I forgot the name of my father, my mother, my country

THE BOOK OF FLESH

In this book there are pieces of flesh; skin and ash and rain and the book is one of many piled in a tower of books in the center of an endless circle of ash. The book we now refer to, the Book of Flesh, was written by a blind man whose eyes were removed for saying the wrong thing to the wrong man at the wrong time and in the wrong place. It is written in the book, in a language of flesh, that the blind man, after having his eyeballs removed, had the empty slots of his eyes filled with worms. And the worms slithered around where his eyes were, and through the worms he could see; they were like eyes for him, and they crawled over his face and lips, and he could see through his lips, and the book of flesh is his story, pieced together in swaths of skin, removed from elbows and knees, from shoulders and knuckles. And towards the end of the book, where the flesh from the man's back twists into birds and stars and butterflies and faces with thick lips and empty eyes, there is a story that the flesh readers call memory: here the flesh words tell of a man who falls out of an airplane, and when his bones splatter each shard of bone forms a country, and in each country there are men who have been destroyed but who have now been reconstructed as walking pieces of flesh formed into the former bodies they once possessed. The flesh men live in the bones and all day they cry for their loves, the loves they left behind, the loves who were forced to push them out of the airplanes by the bigger men with guns so that their last image of life, their last gasp of life, their last snatch of life would be death at the hands of those they love: this is memory as it is written in the Book of Flesh. This is the nation of flesh that jumps off the page and stabs the reader in the tongue and in the eye. To not say, and to not see: this is how the Book of Flesh must be read: Each page of the Book of Flesh dissolves as it is turned, and new flesh pages take their place. To be inside this book is to live in dead fields, to live in the bowels of dead cattle, to live in the caves of dead seas. The flesh word breaks as it is spoken. The holes from the missing words leave craters in the men of flesh. We climb these men to get from one book to another, from one country to another: this is the beginning of the story: the flesh towers: the flesh gravestones: the suns built of dead flesh. We read this book so that it will absorb us. The flesh made word: the barefoot, bare-legged, boneless children drop out of the book like letters falling from a page. The flesh is lightning fast: a mouth of blood, a dirty hair: these are the residents of the nation of the Book of Flesh. We try not to frighten the book. The breath of life is flesh.

FAILURE IN THE IMAGINATION

for Gabriel Gudding

A hummingbird flies into my window.

I pick up the dead body of the hummingbird and fling it into the woods.

There is a splotch of feathers and blood on my window from the dead hummingbird.

A miniscule poet climbs onto the window and writes a poem using the blood of the hummingbird as ink and a feather as pen.

He writes, the duty of poets is to bring down the economy of the United States.

A poet I know wishes Al Qaeda would bomb the building of a poet he does not like.

A poet in New York City, he wants to get rid of all the other poets in New York City, and he hopes a terrorist will do this for him.

Casually wishing an acquaintance be killed by terrorism is an interesting rhetorical strategy, and it is one that it is valued by the miniscule man writing poetry on my window with the blood of a dead hummingbird.

The miniscule man on my window could very well be a woman.

Barbaric writers include both women and men.

Barbaric women writers value the color of blood while barbaric men writers value the texture of blood.

Barbaric hermaphroditic writers most value the taste of blood.

A poet I know says he has a long penis which he attributes to his village whose poets all have long penises.

He is not being sarcastic when he discusses his penis nor is he being sarcastic when he says that in his village a blow job is called a cream mustache.

The miniscule man on my window is a miniscule hermaphrodite with no buttocks and two groins.

He writes: "If rulers refuse to consider poems as crimes, then someone must commit crimes that serve the function of poetry, or texts that possess the resonance of terrorism."

The miniscule hermaphrodite poet on my window is a terrorist whose deepest desire is to turn Manhattan into a giant bowl of milk

The hermaphrodite poet terrorist stands on a small platform above the bowl of milk.

He writes poetry by slicing off the body parts of the citizens of New York City and dumping them in the bowl of milk.

The disembodied hand of a banker and the disembodied hand of a poet fuse into a pantoum on the far edge of the giant bowl of milk that New York City has now become.

From now on all culture will be body parts floating in milk, shouts the minuscule hermaphrodite poet terrorist through his bullhorn.

The leg of a taxi driver forms a T with the arm of an Upper East Side gallery owner.

The conjunction of these two body parts forms the first letter in the sentence: "Terrorism and poetry are two great tastes that taste great together."

Each resident of New York City has been assigned a time to climb the ladder of bones to reach the small platform where the minuscule hermaphrodite poet terrorist will chop off one of his or her body parts.

If the residents of New York City fail to climb the ladder at the assigned time, their house will be destroyed by Al Qaeda.

To reach the ladder of bones you must cross the tunnel and enter New Jersey.

It is a hard climb and your average New Yorker huffs and puffs to get to the top, where she is greeted by an illegal immigrant child who sells bottles of Coca-Cola and candy bars.

An illegal immigrant girl from a nameless country in a featureless part of the world smashes the heads of the residents of New York City with bottles of Coca-Cola.

In her native language, which sounds like the hiss of a snake, she declares that she is using the tools of the oppressor to create a transformative kind of poetry.

She snips the middle finger from *A Chorus Line* dancer and throws it into the giant bowl of milk.

The dancer climbs down to the bottom of the ladder, where a CNN reporter asks him what he thinks of the new poetry.

I see the bowl of milk in my window; it is now subsuming the Statue of Liberty.

Thus it is time to find a lover for the miniscule hermaphrodite who is writing poetry in my window with the feathers and blood of the dead hummingbird who woke me up this morning with a terrifying thud that I mistook for a bomb.

But here is the truth: when the minuscule hermaphrodite terrorist poet falls in love he/she will have to abandon his/her dream of dumping the body parts of the residents of New York City into the giant bowl of milk.

For love is the opposite of poetry, and poetry is the opposite of silence, and love and silence are not equal in this equation.

The hermaphrodite has now fallen in love with another hermaphrodite who is writing a poem in blood on the window of the house across the street.

The miniscule hermaphrodite terrorist poet whispers in my ear: should I choose love, or poetry?

The hermaphrodite lets out a giant poetic fart that makes my entire apartment vibrate.

A poem falls out of his groin and smashes onto the floor of my bedroom.

The poem is a box wrapped with colorful paper and topped with a bright pink ribbon

I untie the ribbon and discover in the box a fortune cookie I immediately bite into.

The fortune says: "An act of terrorism will soon befall your neighborhood."

The fortune cookie tastes like chocolate cake and strawberries.

I bite into the fortune cookie and release the ocean water trapped inside.

A voice cries: I am bound to you by a contractual obligation both visible and invisible at the same time.

I try to respond but my tongue is stuck to the roof of my mouth.

The miniscule hermaphrodite terrorist poet jumps off the window, hops across the floor, climbs up my leg, my chest, my neck, and into my mouth to unclamp my tongue.

Here are three possible endings to this scene:

1. My tongue remains forever attached to the roof of my mouth and the miniscule hermaphrodite terrorist snuggles comfortably against my inner lip until the end of time.

2. My tongue comes crashing down onto the miniscule hermaphrodite and I am able to speak but never again will I have the power to write poetry.

3. The miniscule hermaphrodite terrorist will pull out my tongue and dump it into the bowl of milk which once was New York City.

THE BOOK OF HOLES

The Book of Holes sits amid the graves of writers who died of writing. Their beds went up in flames when they burned every word they ever wrote. And they burned every word they ever wrote simply by writing. The pen across the page was a match against the striker. The Book of Holes was all that was left of the writers who died from writing. It sits atop the Book of Flesh, and it is a small nation that one enters by refusing to speak. There are books that teach us to die, and then there are books that teach us to live in holes, in total solitude, where we can only be saved by writing. Here the books that are written are naked: we read them in darkness; we can only read them when we are blind. There is a story that sits in the middle of the Book of Holes and which is said to explain all of the other books that are contained within the Book of Holes. It is the story of a cardinal that flies into a window; it is the story of the last few minutes of the cardinal's life. In the book the bird is a nation, and when it dies it turns into an airplane and smaller birds drop out of its belly, and they too are nations that cannot stand the uniformity of the world. A nation of barracks where the tears from the tortured bodies drip like ink and when they hit the ground they form towers of books and on the first page of the book that sits atop the tower there is a free citizen of the world who asks to be chained to the spine of the Book of Holes. I will die on the day that the Book of Holes turns into its opposite, she says, which is to say that for the characters who populate the Book of Holes paradise is to be locked inside the earth and prevented from crawling out of the ground. And so the characters in the Book of Holes speak about bombs to destroy paradise, but the bombs are not bombs, they are minuscule insects with the power to turn earth into ash. Let us now turn to the last page of the Book of Holes. The words on this page have been punctured and all that is left is a fingernail's worth of white paper which itself is filled with the tiniest of holes that are said to have been made by daring red ants. Some say these holes tell the story of she who dared to write the Book of Holes, which begins as a wall: a wall of words about the history of walls that was written by a blind woman who had never seen or touched a wall. She did not know what a wall was, and she did not know what a hole was, and because she knew neither hole nor wall she was able to build a Book of Holes from a torn down Book of Walls. In other words, like most writers, the moment she could write about what she wrote about what she wrote about ceased to exist. And it is terrifying to read the Book of Holes just as it is terrifying to sit in the rubble of the Book of Walls and to write about death but to never be able to die. It is only in the Book of Holes that the story of the destruction of the Book of Walls can be endurable. For in the rubble there are lilies, and in the lilies there are countries, and they too are books: warm-bodied books that live in a wasteland of roots.

STATE POETRY

This poem was written in the office of a state employee, and typed on a state-owned computer, and as such it is a violation of state ethics rules which prevent state employees from using state resources for work that is beyond the employee's job description.

Because this poem was written on a state-owned computer, and printed on a state-owned printer, and copied on a state-owned Xerox machine, it is, by law, the property of the state.

This poem willfully submits itself to state ownership.

This poem feels that there is no better owner of a poem than the state.

This poem feels that state-controlled poetry is the poetry of the future

When the author of this poem is appointed Poet Laureate of Illinois, this poem will instantly transform into an important work of literature.

This poem has an active staff of fundraisers who are seeking corporate sponsorship.

This poem is static, and in the stasis of this poem, a community of poets shall be blown to ash by a force that believes in art as a government and military weapon.

This poem speaks of the world, but in its attempt to speak of the world it is interrupted by bureaucrats writing poetic memos; by generals writing poetic death orders; by refugees writing poetic love songs to sheep, Israeli Uzis, and virgins.

This poem carries guns, prayer books, maps, cash, and manuals for heavy machinery.

This poem contains poet-interrogators who shove into terrorist mouths a variety of sedatives in preparation for gradual neurological reprogramming.

This poem is to be read through a walkie-talkie at a convention of poets who long to be institutionalized.

This poem institutionalizes poets by granting them immediate tenure at state universities they will never be able to leave.

In the world of this poem, a ball of dust is a Neanderthal man with a club; a cobweb is a poppy field full of landmines; and a horse on a road is fourteen illegal immigrants in a stable.

Critics hate this poem.

Editors laugh at this poem.

Poets shit on this poem.

Babies and graduate students eat this poem.

There are bivalved mollusks in this poem, and hemorrhoids, and a dog named Chucho, and coyotes who kidnap immigrants.

This poem speaks of a sheepherder's wife in the same breath that it mentions a cheerleader from the Upper East Side who fashions pom-poms from the hair of poodles captured by her Canine Detention Brigade.

This poem is an ally of the Metrosexual Insurgents who waged war on Banana Republic after maxing out their credit cards.

This poem is actively recruiting insurgents to terrorize exurban outlet malls.

This poem is a representative sample of the Chilean-Jewish school of Western Pennsylvanian Poetics.

This poem is rhythmically unappealing.

The form of this poem has little to do with its content.

This poem longs to be doused in gasoline and shoved into the mouths of enemy combatants at Guantanamo Bay.

This poem has no desire to withstand the test of time, and its author recommends that all copies of this poem be burned two years after publication.

This poem is firm in its convictions and compassionate at the same time.

This is a people-poem, not a political poem.

This poem is committed to public service.

This poem is simple, unobtrusive, and easy to use or ignore as the reader sees fit.

THE READERS

Who reads these books? Or more appropriately, who are the characters in these books who read these books? For these books exist: they are nations in a prison filled with other nations that would do anything to be something other than nations, other than books. Let us describe our readers. Their fingers have been pulled off by doctors who specialize in removing the fingers from the residents of dead nations and making it seem as if these disembodied fingers are like leaves falling from the sky. The fingers were stuck in pages of books: the Book of Fingers is a nation we will soon come to. It sits in the memory folds, in the sand dunes that run through the tower of books and which are themselves small nations. The fingers: they are pasted in the pages of books and their owners flip through these books by using their mouths, toes, elbows, and shoulders. Some of the readers have lost their tongues and those tongues are also in books: The Book of Tongues, a favorite of the blind readers who populate the nations, tells the story of how the readers lost their tongues: they were forced to bite off their own tongues in a competition to see who could bite off their own tongue the fastest. The winner got to keep his tongue, which was sewn back on; the losers had their tongues memorialized in books. The air is thick with pollution in the nation where the readers live. Fingers and tongues and eyeballs and arms fall from the sky and there are no more insects because of the chemicals sprayed over the cities. The readers live in the mountains above the tower of books and they descend every few weeks to make sure their tongues and fingers have not been removed. They know this verification they embark upon is nostalgia at its worse, and when they trip over the littered body parts they are relieved that these are not actually humans. The dead humans tossed from airplanes fill the canals just as the dead rain fills the canals and the dead snow fills the canals and the dead soil fills the canals and the dead skin and the dead hair and the dead milk and the dead sand on the dead beaches of the dead ocean. The readers of these books are Sirens: they are so beautiful they attract nobody. They have sterile wombs and they are chained to mountains and the only thing they attract are books. The readers do not come to the books. On the contrary, the books come to the readers the way diplomats line up to pay tribute to dead heads of state. The readers flip through the books with their tongues and though they do not look for themselves in the books they are there, stuck to each page, gyrating, pulsating, weeping. Stuck to the books they stare up at their tongue-less mouths and they wish to leap inside their own bellies which are also countries. And the tongues and the fingers that are glued to the pages murmur when they see their own bodies. And from the tower of books there comes an endless murmur which from a distance sounds like marching boots but when one comes closer to the tower of books one realizes that the murmur is itself a form of architecture, and that the tower is itself a form of architecture, and that the dead fingers are a city and that in this city populated by readers there are thousands of voices that do not belong to bodies: this murmur is memory and the murmur is the dead ocean and its opposite and it will forever and always be blank.

BETWEEN HOLE-WORD AND WORD-WORD

to seize hold of a memory as it flashes up at a moment of danger...

– WALTER BENJAMIN
(translated by Harry Zohn)

The poem begins with a refugee boy unscrewing his wrist and jumping through the screen of a Power Point presentation in the office of a nameless bureaucrat.

The poem continues with the refugee boy declaring to the bureaucrats: "my body has turned to mud."

In the next line the refugee boy unscrews his leg, and in the hollows of his flesh there is a river, and at the end of the first stanza the boy who has turned to mud leaps into the river.

Power needs only power to justify itself, reads the next slide in the Power Point presentation, which is the next line of the poem.

The line shifts to an image of a river carrying the boy through the "o" in power, but the boy hangs onto the upper edge of the "o" and in so doing he resists the sweep of history.

In the next line the reader hears a mechanized female voice reciting the following words:

"Because the imagination industry keeps failing to predict the future, we are in the future now, we are in the future now."

And in the next line all the bureaucrats chant: "We are in the future now, we are in the future now."

And so as to better understand the future, the bureaucrats, at the beginning of the third stanza, memorize *Tyger! Tyger! burning bright!*

And in the next line the bureaucrats express great empathy for the refugee boy, who informs them through subliminal messages that he was put on this earth for no other reason than to suffer.

I am trying to avoid lyricism, the speaker states parenthetically, and hopefully I have been successful, but I am hindered by the fact that every few lines or so blood drips from the boy's stumpy arm into a sonorous puddle of ghost voices.

And in the next line, the bureaucrats, who definitively are not barbarians, stride gracefully through the puddle of blood and into the virulent poetic muck where they are forced to enter their data.

In the next line a bureaucrat sits by the river, calculating modern horrors with an abacus.

He speaks of fish floating up from the sea, of birds falling out of the sky.

He speaks of fish and birds, but the reader knows he is speaking of humans from the way he dips his finger in blood and draws circles on the side of his face.

The poem approaches the end, an open end where the water, in the voice of Marguerite Duras, murmurs that we have reached a transitional station between word-word and hole-word.

The poem wishes to end, but it still needs to convey some vital information to the refugee boy who earlier unscrewed his wrist for the sake of poetry:

Son, do not speak the hole-word because if you speak the hole-word you will ruin all other words.

Son, do not murmur the names of the dead because if you murmur the names of the dead you will ruin the poetry of death.

Son, when you get to the sanatorium, make a final request: do not let them take your soul from your body unless you have a contractual agreement that your soul will live forever.

THE BOOK OF LOVERS

One pulls this book out of the tower of books and on the first page, the epigraph, written with shards of glass and swirls of ash, directs the reader to go to the mountain. Here is your ticket to the mountain, says the first page of the Book of Lovers. When you get there you will find a cave and in that cave you will find a lake and in that lake you will find that the water has practically dissolved and all that is left are the lovers. They are shells on the floor of the lake. They are snails and clams and worms and parasites on the floor of the lake. And of course there are bones. They are everywhere. And the reader of the Book of Lovers, on arriving at the lake, knows, without being told, that she must arrange the bones to form a bridge, a bridge to nowhere, some might say, and it is true that the bridge is suspended from one wall of the cave and it does not stretch to the other, but when one runs their fingers over the bridge one hears the call of the lovers: a murmur, a body drowning in mud and quicksand and a voice that murmurs I loved you when the country was alive, I loved you when I was more than a ghost stuck in this purgatory because the preachers had no standing to bless us into heaven. I loved you when the lovers wore fingers, when the lovers wore tongues, when the limbs of the lovers were not pasted in books. I loved you and in our love we exploded and ran through the living fields of lilies and sunflowers and there were babies in our arms and our huts overlooked lakes and we swam with the other lovers until the God-men came with their guns and machetes to slash off our tongues and fingers. My love, I don't own my words now, they sit in the slots of the barbed-wire fence and they sit in the electric chairs and in the gurneys and in the guillotines and in the eyes of the lovers who wait for their blows with love and fear and honor. My love, my words are in the flames where the lovers dance and which the lovers are forced to stick the hands and feet of their lovers into. The reader of the Book of Lovers is a reader of voices. With each flip of the page there is a murmur of a ghost-voice of a lover who once lived to love and who loved the words and the sky and the water and the bread and the stones and the sounds on which their lovers tread. The Book of Lovers vibrates and buzzes and when the reader holds it her hands tremble; some say they burn, and some say the book glows, and some say if you hold the Book of Lovers long enough the water will refill the lake in the cave in the mountains and once more the snow will start to live. Those who have read the book say this but it is said that when they speak these words a stream of petroleum gushes from their mouths and one can't help but strike a match and set the book and the world aflame.

IN MY NUMB HEART, A PRICK OF MISGIVING

I want a poet who can be toilet trained to prevent the shit from spilling out of his mouth.

If you can't feel the tickle on your genitals that this poem provides, please contact the manufacturer.

I like to cuddle. I am loyal and intelligent. And I will sell myself for the mere thrill of seeing my name on a bathroom wall, or anagrammatically in the pages of *Paradise Lost*.

I do not own this poem; it is the responsibility of the poetic community.

If you cannot sex this poem, then listen harder.

The wind has fallen.

The words don't know what they mean.

Four out of five poets complain they are jealous of new arrivals.

The best poet in our town lives in a cage at *Pets'R'Us* and says fuck the son of a bitch every time a customer walks by.

I prefer the jargon of capitalists to the jargon of poets.

I love the word: "liquidity."

I love the world: "asset."

I learned from television that the area between the testicles and the anus is called the runway.

She slid her finger along his runway and read from the *Cantos* of Ezra Pound:

That profit on deposits should be used to cover all losses and the distributions of the fifth year be made from remaining profits after restoration of losses no matter how small with the sane small reserve against future idem, and so on.

I believe in the rapture of syntax, and I take no responsibility if this poem suddenly falls into a coma, or if the economy of the poetry market experiences bloated bouts of inflation due to the overvalued chunks of language that glitter like diamonds in the glistening pool of vomit that spreads across the floor like the shadow of a lover long forgotten.

The poet scared her own children with her excruciatingly meticulous word choice.

She exhibited aggressive behavior in public when she recited her serventesios.

Her best poem consisted of three hundred and fifteen gaseous staccato eruptions.

The emcee suggested that disappointed consumers contact the manufacturer.

The poet was lifted from the tenure track and dumped onto the customer service desk at Home Depot.

The poet went bust but the bank took over the practice.

THE BOOK OF GLASS

It is impossible to read the Book of Glass without spilling blood. The reader pulls it out of the tower with special tongs and sets it on the ground. A dagger sticks out of the cover and it is stained with the blood of previous readers. Smaller glass daggers stick out of the larger dagger making it impossible to touch any point on the larger dagger without wounding hands. The blood against the yellow and purple glass of the larger and smaller daggers, when hit by sunlight, is stunning to the eye. You will have to take my word for this: it's so beautiful it causes the reader to lose her senses and she can't help but try to open the book. The reader grabs for the cover, and the blood that is then drawn forms the text of the book, which is filled with the blood of previous readers. The reader's blood swirls across these first pages and the blood informs us that the text is about writing itself: here the writers are readers and they have gone too far with their own mortality. They die to read, die to write, and in the blood that swirls around the page and mixes with the blood of previous writers and readers there is the image of a massacre: the readers are rounded up by a God-man and some are forced into rocks and some into caves and some into mountains and some into rivers; and the water and earth and grass and leaves and air are dead and filled with the murmurs of the lovers who wait for that silence where thought refuses to think. To die to read, to die to write: the Book of Glass is a constant reminder that when people die their words unravel, flow out of their mouths like poison, and when their words hit the earth the soil loses all of its nutrients, the rivers dry up and the readers are thirsty. Or so it says in the Book of Glass, whose final chapter, written with the sharp edges of broken bottles, tells of a man who dreams of his own death in the pages of the Book of Glass. In this tale the Book of Glass is enormous, and the man is tiny in comparison. He needs a crane to help him open the cover, and when he finally gets it open he hops onto a page. On one corner of the page, there is a tower of sharp glass, which reads: in order to continue you must climb this tower. The man hoists himself onto the tower, and with each step he takes blood is drawn from his feet, hands, legs, chest, arms, and fingers. The blood drips down the tower, wells up on the page between the deadly glass formations and coagulates into a sentence that says something along the lines of: the book will end when there are no longer any readers; your job, dear reader, is to disappear to make the words possible, to make the blood possible, to make the destruction of the book possible, and this can only occur if you live forever and die on this page at the same time. The man continues to climb the tower of glass and as he climbs he feels himself becoming a parable about a parable that does not know if it is reality or parable. He lives like this for many decades until finally he forgets about himself, which is to say that in the final scene birds carry him away and drop him in a field of strawberries or sunflowers, where he forever murmurs the question: what is the weight of light?

LOVE IN THE TIME OF POETRY

We listened to the poetry of infestation, and from above a giant appendage dug out the pestilence from between my toes, and the fungal poets scampered into the fingernail of a well-versed critic, and the verses swarmed and reproduced around any old mouth that belched or wept or driveled.

I recited Baudelaire on the gurney, and as the professor dug his nail into my back the miniscule poets crawled across my body, and as meaning spat through his fluids into my fluids, I heard a critic detailing my flaws: my mature cells were not being released from the fatty tissue in the inside of my bones; my veins were too fragile; waste products and fluids were building up at dangerous levels. In short, my organism could not achieve stability through adaptation or change; the miniscule poets in my skin repelled the miniscule poets in his skin. I felt pain where there was no pain, feeling where there was no feeling.

He offered me a canto, a rispetto, a serventesio.

I begged my molecules to link together.

I said: do you not have a drug that can make my muscles contract?

Meantime, in the salons: gun shots and explosions; cats in heat howling in a three-story tower of trash. The poets in the trash, imploding, and glass blowing out of storefront windows, and in the rubble the origin of a stanza: the putrefaction of a silent word, a believer pre-empting God with the decision to write, to read, to fill a space with echoes.

The echoes were trapped; the animal technology sterilized.

The organism raised its hand over the poet's mouth, but shit dribbled through my fingers.

I'm a poor little canker, said the professor, as he scooted down the hog hose of politics and into the esotericism of rhythm.

Brussels, Vienna, Paris, London, New York, San Francisco, Buenos Aires: yesterday's lyricism was groaning like a dead man praying to the horse who flung him off his back and stomped him to bile. The rider-less horse galloped through the dirt trails of the flesh tunnel. A haggard sense of meaning: a transcendent son of a bitch is like that.

A leper; the unsayable syllable: love. Hallelujah shouted the poet-beasts who swallowed their own hearts as if they were stir-fried giblets.

And in the pile of slush, the only one left was the critic. He stood on a mound of entrails, barfed into his blog, and said:

If you piss for me, if you relieve me of the responsibility of having to piss for the rest of my life, I'll fill your sonnet with stocks and bonds.

When he emptied his bladder, he emptied my bladder, and in so doing I felt the dissolution of the means of production:

The earth dissolved into text. The text dissolved into station.

THE BOOK OF GRAVES

Writing is learning to die. It's learning not to be afraid, in other words
to live at the extremity of life, which is what the dead, death, give us.

– HÉLÈNE CIXOUS
(translated by Sarah Cornell and Susan Sellers)

The Book of Graves is buried beneath the tower of books. To find it the
reader must dig, she must use the other books as shovels, she must dig with
her hands and feet, and hide in shadows so that the sun will not burn her.
There are few trees near the tower of books, and those that still stand have
dead leaves, but at certain times of day the books themselves cast shadows,
and we who read must constantly move in order to stay safe from the sun,
which in the Book of Books burns the limbs off readers, off writers, off
residents who live in the world of images, of ghosts, of dreams. Dig for
the Book of Graves, the signs say, and you will find it next to a ladder that
helps you move from one book to another, from one country to another,
from one bloody word to another. Don't climb up the ladder, the words
say, you'll dissolve into the earth; but if the ladder lets you descend, then
by all means, descend, and take the Book of Graves with you, and wait for
something to happen, anything—an ant to crawl, a volcano to erupt—and
soon enough the third chapter of the grave that is the Book of Graves will
open its lid, and you will crawl in, and you will be with the dead, or you will
be dead, and the smell of putrefaction will itself be a story. Yes, the Book of
Graves is written in odors: this is the smell of the holy book as it is bathed

in excrement and shoved into the hands of the bearded man who screams for his mother and country and who thinks he now is a palm tree or a bit of a rust on a barbed-wire fence: there are countries in his beard: countries of dead hairs that smell of wedding preparations in a country of rubble, a country where the ancient implodes and the modern implodes and the body parts that fall from the sky smell like vinegar; they split open as they fall and more countries fall out of them and the dead countries smell like wet rugs whose shags shelter the last spasms of birds and grasshoppers, lizards, and frogs. And the smell of decomposition forms words which involuntarily leap onto pages and form voices, murmurs from a purgatory that is far worse than hell; and the page flips and there are odors: here is the smell of an old, wet, leather binding to a book wherein the dead who do not believe in life after death moan in resentment; here is the smell of blood that has mixed with ink and formed rivers from which fish ascend into a sea-sky where the algae weighs hundreds of pounds and there in the sky on the edge of the horizon the hair burns and the shoes burn and the skin burns off those bodies who were promised that death is sudden but instead it is a long shower of hail and words and words and hail and the hail and the words are interchangeable just as the gas and the electricity are interchangeable and the lightning and the sun are interchangeable and the rivers and the trees are interchangeable. The residents of the Book of Graves are monsters: they are like people who forgot to stop breathing when they die. They breathe and forget, they breathe and forget: the odor of life and memory.

THE ROCKET

for Mark Piper, Thomas Kuhn, Severo Sarduy

The sky disappears into the dirt that is covering my ears.

You can see the rocket taking off long before you hear it.

The event itself, the launching of the rocket, disappears into the mud that is
    swallowing my face.

Normally, my face swallows the mud, but today it is different.

Today the mud swallows my face.

Today my face disappears into a device that receives a signal in the form of
    one type of energy and converts it to a signal in another type of energy.

My face converts acoustic energy into electrical impulses.

Worms crawl into my face in order to measure the sensitivity of the
    electrical systems that have gathered in my mouth.

Worms disappear into my nose as the image appears in the mud.

The rocket.

It emerges from the southern swamp at the back of my throat.

Four types of federally listed endangered species live in my mouth.

The Salt Marsh Snake, the Piping Plover, the American Alligator and the
    Leatherback Turtle.

They are in my mouth with the worms and the rocket is taking off into space.

I have witnessed the largest celestial explosion any man has ever seen.

It happened in my face, in the sinews deep in my nose, in the small tubes
    that connect parts of me to other parts of me that I cannot explain and
    that I do not wish to know about.

The rocket.

It emerges from a small hole at the corner of my lips.

It is much like vomiting, but the information, the information that flows
from the lungs to the throat, from the throat to the teeth, from the
teeth to the tongue, from the tongue to the lips, is different.

The information that flows out of my mouth when I spit out the rocket is a
device that consists of the junction of two dissimilar metallic conductors.

It is aphrodisiacal.

My mouth is full of copper and my tongue is full of iron.

The electromotive force in my mouth is induced when the conductors are
maintained at different temperatures.

Some call this science and others call it music.

The information here is horrible.

How vague.

The formation, the interpolation, the interleaving telemetry, the blank leaves
in the book, the integration of electrical translation through a third
substance that connects to the junction of resistive thermal force:
it is the body that breathes in my mouth.

My love I swallowed you and in my mouth the information that you became
filled my teeth like rockets in a sea-fire, like rockets landing on the
minuscule bony plates that cross the carapace from the anterior to the
posterior margin of the turtle's leathery back.

We converge.

You and I converge in my mouth and in the sky.

We converge in my mouth and in the sky and we disappear in my mouth
and in the sea.

We disappear with the rocket.

We disappear with the rocket as it disappears in the sky and in the sea.

The music of information that accompanies the disappearing rocket.

The information flowing. It's like bodies.

Dancing bodies pairing off with one another, filled with fiery, metallic information.

The bodies: they are identical in form and structure.

The air is thick with them.

The air of the sky and the air of my mouth and the air of the sea is thick
   with them.

They converge.

They converge in my mouth and in the sky and in the sea.

They converge to gather information, to measure information, to collect
   and interpret data.

My body is an accelerometer that measures the vibrations of your body.

My body is a controlled explosion that is an offspring from a controlled
   explosion in another body.

I push out of the skin of another body the way the rocket pushes out of the
   skin of the earth and into the curve of the air.

There is silence as you escape the earth's atmosphere.

There is silence as the air gets thinner and the universe gets darker and darker.

What orbits the satellite must be placed into a room full of consoles.

Zero. Zero. Zero. Zero. One.

Zero. Zero. Zero. Zero. One.

The room full of consoles is manned by a room full of bureaucrats who
   wish to see a commercial mission pass through my mouth through the
   sea through the air and into outer space.

I am interested in the acoustics of this.

I am interested in the air pressure, in the dullness of this.

I am interested in the things that fall out of my mouth and off the body of
   the rocket as it leaves the earth.

I am interested in the incommensurability of competing paradigms of space.

I shall explicate further.

In my mouth is a flat, curved, matrix of space.

I live in a different world.

You live with me.

I see different things in different relations one to the other.

You see a rocket. I see a lover in my mouth.

You see a transition between incommensurables and I see a transition
between logic and natural experience.

Blood and hair fall off the rocket as it leaves my mouth and sinks into the earth.

A body blooms and dissolves in the network of light that dies as the rocket
leaves the sea and enters the air and sky.

Here is the rocket that falls from the sky while searching for another rocket
that holds in its storage system information that leads eventually to
certain slips of paper that lead eventually to an even larger storage
system that leads to a series of codes and passwords that are contained
in other storage systems that can only be accessed by certain bodies
who know how to speak certain words and in the proper combination.

Did I mention I sleep in a bed that is much too small for my body?

Did I mention I live in a mouth that is much too small for my teeth?

Did I mention I live in a swampy marsh that is much too large for the
murmurs that consume us as we listen to the dying of the sand, to
the dying of the moon, to the disappearance of white stones, to the
reversal of light, to the absorption and emission of the forest the sky
and the sea?

These facts need further emphasis.

Nevertheless, the key is to write the same book and to write in different
ways every time.

Similarly, the key is to leave the atmosphere in the same way and to leave
　　differently every time.
A community of scientific specialists will do everything it can to ensure the
　　continued growth of the assembled data just as a lover will do it everything
　　it can to ensure the continued growth of its controlled explosions.
We were afraid that we could not control the temperature devices that
　　linked us together.
The paradigm shifted.
The composite signal previously created by the commutation process is
　　like the composite signal created by the trail of those searching for
　　the bodies that have disappeared, which are compatible with the blank
　　signals and the burnt skin in my cheek, which are compatible with the
　　nebulous pulsation that my mouth produces as it sinks into the earth
　　and dies.

THE BOOK OF ECHOES

The reader who opens the Book of Echoes finds a village where no one lives and nothing grows and where all the houses are empty. A famished-looking man meets the reader at the entrance to the village. I know that you came to find the Book of Echoes, says the man, who now takes the reader on a tour through the village, but it is gone. It has vanished. Or better said, the Book of Echoes is indistinguishable from the living echoes that the ghost-men and the god-men intone as they search for an exit from purgatory. A few flips of the pages and soon the book disappears and there are ghost-men and God-men who march through the village looking for an audience to hear what they have to peddle. A man opens his mouth and a little bomb drops out of it and when it detonates books and rivers form out of the ashes. The reader opens a page from one of the new books that has been birthed by the bomb. On the first page there is a country and everyone in it smiles. They are not happy but the law says they must smile or their teeth and lips will be ripped from their faces. They smile and sob at the same time and their sobs echo and the little bombs that fall from the mouths of the writers and readers echo and the silence echoes and the tour guide who brought the reader into the Book of Echoes says to the reader: It's been a long time since you've been gone. You have been here before; this village hides in another village in another book that you have previously entered. A bomb falls out of the tour guide's mouth and thousands of poems spill out and there is a desert and there are bones that tell stories of the families who live on the margins of this book: they are parables, sure, but they too drop bombs out of their mouths and from their armpits and they store bombs in their knees and they fling bombs with their fingers and toes. And the bombs are like poems and rain and static and the horns of buses and trucks; and they fill the smiles of the citizens; and the echoes of the bombs are like little blessings that teach us how to blow up all the lies that have taught us to live. Yes the bombs in this book are blessings and the citizens smile at them and sob and there are cities on the horizon exploding and bodies falling from airplanes and the bodies buzz when the reader holds them to her chest and in the vibration of the lifeless bodies there is one long oooooooooooooooooooooooooooooo; and the moment the ooooooooooooooooooooooo ends the reader finds a mirror and in the glass there is a baby breathing in a field and in the bomb that is the baby's cry there is breath and more breath and there is the memory of the time when the citizens of the village did not smile instead they wore sadness on their faces and they laughed and there were words written in the river, and the river said grow and smile and don't smile, and there was a leg that floated into the picture and it was a prayer and we tossed it to the citizens and they smiled and read the leg and held it to their cheeks and it echoed across the entire village and the citizens laid down to die in the beds where they were born but they could not die; they could only sob and murmur and smile.

BUDGET CUTS PREVENT ME
FROM WRITING POETRY

You say I wish to create a universe that is an insane asylum

But I am only one American and the planets are all on Quaaludes

And the baby is in the bassinet and the eggs are in their baskets

And the semen are in their testicles and Hamlet is a faceless robot who is president of the rotary

And the myth where I am dying from abuse of language

Is ascending and descending at the same time

I'd tear myself to shreds to prevent you from calling me a poet

Or even an anti-poet for I am the apropos of nothing

And I am the check this box for all of the above

And I am a smudged-out image of Joan of Arc praying in a toxic rainstorm

And I am in myself more than I know myself

And me and I are the ideal couple

And as we seduce each other we think of Kim Jong-Il making love to a Swedish prostitute in a barbed-wire cage

And we think of vital organs for sale on eBay

And we refuse to Google ourselves because we do not want to know what the world thinks of the binary system we have become

And we think of monads and visual simulacra

And Daffy Duck is a gigantic tarantula crawling through the famished roads of ambiguity, where a bearded man with bulging pockets asks if I'm a poet

I vomit a poem onto a stack of bloody cows and win a Pushcart Prize

And for a split second nothing stays the same until we flail into the simile of history

THE BOOK OF EXPECTATIONS

What do we expect from the books? Or better said, what do the readers who find the books in the tower of books expect from them? For when one reads about blood and brains and mountains and rivers and deserts and body parts that fall from the sky surely one must think about the reality actually in the books versus the reality one expects to find in the books. We turn, of course, to another book to address this question. It is the Book of Expectations, a parasite dug deep in the other books. After a long search the reader opens the Book of Expectations and the first page is a ladder that carries her down to the sand dune. Remember, the ladders in the Books do not ascend; they only descend, thus when the reader gets to the bottom she will need to find another book to bring her back up, but that's a different story, a different book, a different sun and a different night. The reader climbs down the pages of the Book of Expectations and lands in the sand dune. The sand dune is a country and its citizens are stuck in books; they refuse to live in the light, in the rain, in the grass, and in valleys. You know these people, you are one of them, and so you know what happens when our reader gets to the bottom of the dunes: she can't sleep. She can't even imagine herself sleeping. We leaf through the Book of Expectations and we are with her on every page, not sleeping. In the darkness we hear noises: here is the buzz of the electric chair; here is the buzz of the razor as it shaves the head of the man who sits in the electric chair; here is the sound of the breath of the barber who shaves the head of the man who sits in the electric chair; here is the sound of body ABC ordering the obliteration of body XYZ. Here is the engine of the airplane as body XYZ is flown above the sea; here is the sound of the spoon stirring the poison that will be administered to body XYZ.

Here is the last gasp from body XYZ; here is the breeze as body XYZ cuts through the sky on its descent into the desert. Here is the sound that body XYZ makes when it lands in the desert. Here is the sound of the country that forms when body XYZ's arms fall off and spills their blood. Here are the citizens of the country that march out of the blood of the severed arm of body XYZ. Here are the vultures and buzzards, the coyotes and owls, the rattle snakes and lizards; here are the desert critters that drink the blood of body XYZ. This is the Book of Expectations: it is every sound we hear when we do not sleep; it is no more than a reminder of how little there is to say, to think, and to feel. To read and to live, to live and to read. The book is the body that inhabits you, dear reader; but it is not your body. It is blood that drips in the night.

IN OTHER WORDS

The boy I allegedly kicked in the face doesn't have a face. And if he did have a face, why would he stick it beneath my foot, which I do not have. And if I did have a foot, why would it kick, when it could dance or tap or twitch.

I walk on crutches, a sock over my stump to keep my blood from leaking, though sometimes my blood leaks, and when it leaks it coagulates, and when it coagulates I turn into a brick, and I rest between other bricks because I do not have the language to pull myself apart, and to fall into the fortified city where all the poets are gangsters, where all the bankers are poets, and where the only difference between a banker and a gangster is their approach to rhythm and syntax.

There is a rooster that pecks at this wall. He thinks he's a dog. He howls; he pisses on this wall in which I am but a brick, this wall that prevents me from seeing how the words I write prevent me from rotting, prevent my dust from mingling, properly, into the yellow dust of war.

Without the art of exaggeration, the war would be dull. We would watch it from our homes, noting its alchemy the way one notes the screech of a distant bird before sunset. And the screech of a distant bird before sunset would be nothing more than an occasion to write an occasional poem about what we hear but do not see, about what we see but do not perceive, about what we perceive but do not know.

Everything that ends as poetry begins as blood and infamy.

THE BOOK OF FORGOTTEN BODIES

The reader who opens the Book of Forgotten Bodies finds nothing. There are no horses galloping through deserted villages in search of the men who used to ride them. There are no children crying for their parents who were thrown out of airplanes and into the sea. There are no soldiers who had their arms sliced off for refusing to obliterate innocent bodies. There are no rich men leaning against paradise trees as the drunk bodies of poor men stumble up to their houses to kill them. There are no bodies of hopeless virgins smashed on city streets by Mercedes-Benzes cruising through the gentle drizzle of a foggy day. There are no bodies abandoned on beaches. There are no corpses floating down rivers. There are no bodies hanging in the military barracks on island XYZ off the coast of nation ABC. There are no bodies that pound rock against rock. No bodies that stand on one leg with hoods over their mouths mumbling words we don't understand. No bodies covered in mud murmuring to the bodies who lie on top of them. There are no bodies that smell of chemicals and rest in puddles in the rain waiting for flowers to fall on their heads. No blind bodies that are painted by artists who value aesthetics over breath. No bodies that imagine their children's bodies as ghosts and cadavers and skeletons. No bodies that live in bodies that no longer know if they are bodies. No bodies that fall from windows as they try to catch glimpses of the bodies that have fallen before them. There are no bodies discovered by rabid dogs in houses abandoned before they could even be built. No bodies surrounded by barbed wire as the countries die in the distance. No bodies whose skin burns in the strange machines that buzz like tropical nights. No bodies that burn in buildings that have been set on fire by bodies with no reason to live. There are no bodies that fry in the sun, that drown in the shadows, that roast on gas, that ooze algae and moss, that are covered in black rags as the lakes and the mountains die. No bodies that hunt or are hunted, that murder out of charity, that are murdered out of charity. No bodies that shutter the windows and hang themselves in libraries of their favorite books. There are no soulless bodies, no frozen bodies, no bodies gnawed to death by insects. There are no practical bodies, no transient bodies, no empty bodies, no blank bodies that twist between forgotten body and dream.

ONE SIZE FITS ALL

See that immigrant freezing beneath the bridge: he needs a blanket.

See that Torah scroll from the 16th century: it sprawls on the floor like a deadbeat; the Jews need to wrap it in a schmatte.

The problem, you see, is "exposure."

The poet forgot to shake off his penis and pee dripped on the manuscript that he submitted to the 2007 University of Iowa Poetry Prize.

The literary scholar took off his tie and lectured the class on the post-humanoid implications of the virtual cocktail.

He put a pistol on his desk and told the students he was going to kill himself if they didn't do their homework.

Everything in his "worldview" was exposed.

The data-entry specialist imagined new forms for the senior administrator who was only a temporary carcass, an anti-poem: a budding literary movement that communed with master works by committing suicide while reading them.

The temporary carcass of the bureaucrat, dry as Vietnamese Jerky, called out for "gravy" as it "peppered" the eloquent field of syntax.

Abrupt exposure to ordinary language may result in seriously compromised intelligence, implied the carcass as he lipped the trembling lily which hid the police officer, who said: if you look at me one more time I'm going to zap you with my Taser gun.

Abrupt exposure to gateway bureaucracy may result in apocalyptic equivocation, implied the carcass as he dreamed of nomadic man-eaters with a language all their own.

I liked the former "Language Poet" for the speech act he attached to the back of my book, which reminded me of Charles Olson on human growth hormones.

The problem, said the critic, remains one of imagination and its insistence on the distinction between thought and action.

"I let him touch my wooden leg," she said, "and when I unscrewed it I was stuck legless in the hay."

Which is to say that the detachable penis is was and has always been compatible with family values.

"He was a seriously hardworking boy with a fetish for glass eyes and wooden legs," she said, "and I really really loved him."

The poetry era reached its nadir as the housing market plummeted, said the professor, as he repeated for the umpteenth time the anecdote about the boy who met an underwater woman as old as the hills.

"Does Poetry live here," he asked. "Poetry lives here," she replied, "but he will chop you up and kill you, and then he'll cook you and eat you."

My ideal reader has neither a name, a body, nor an online profile.

Which is not to say that I am not concerned with customer satisfaction.

Dear Reader, Because we value your input, please take a moment of your busy time to answer the following question, which will greatly assist us in our mission to produce cultural artifacts that will further meet your aesthetic and spiritual needs.

Which of these statements most accurately reflects your feelings about the writing you have just read:

a) This is a splendid poem, distinguished by the clarity of its thought, the force of its argument, and the eloquence of its expression.

b) This poem is conceptually vapid, artistically shallow, and contributes nothing to the world of letters. It is little more than a collection of bad sentences and poorly formed ideas.

c) I like this poem, but I wouldn't spend money to read more poems like it.

d) When I read this poem, I feel frustrated and annoyed.

e) When I read this poem, I feel nothing.

THE BOOK OF BROKEN BODIES

The Book of Broken Bodies is itself a broken book. The cover is torn; the pages are ripped out; and the ink has smeared so that the words can no longer be read. But the images and photographs are more or less clear, and they depict the various bodies that have been found broken in the desert and on the beaches and in the mountains and in the rivers and hanging in the barracks and buried in the mud and trapped in the holes where the rats and dogs have devoured them. In the Book of Broken Bodies the bodies meld together in a tangle of flesh and blood and mucus. Here the men with no tongues walk arm-in-arm with the women whose genitals have been electrocuted. Here the bodies who drank themselves silly and sliced off their fingers whisper with the prison guards who hold sacs of hands and toes that were taken from the men before they were forced to bark like dogs as they hobbled alone in the night. Here the hair of the men and women they burned sits atop the men and women they saved, and the hair of the men and women they saved has been collected and formed into towers of hair to remind the prisoners of what will never return. A train runs through the final page of the Book of Broken Bodies. It slices off a leg of a prisoner and the leg is picked up by a one-armed man who collects the body parts that once belonged to his friends and neighbors. And what of the citizens whose bodies were broken from writing? They are hands and fingers and arms that hide in the Book of Broken Bodies. They are words that the reader can only utter when she herself becomes an image in the Book of Broken Bodies. Flip through the pages of the book and the body parts become more and more like blades and daggers that serve no purpose but to slice off more body parts and to string them throughout the country where they hang on flag poles in front of hospitals whose patients are searching for their limbs. Yes, the Book of Broken Bodies is a substitute for another book that the authors were too scared to write. Nevertheless, in its aesthetic and moral failure, the Book of Broken Bodies says more about the sky and the fields and the alleys and the sewers than all of the other books combined.

POETRY IS DANGEROUS IN AMERICA

The dangling participle smashed into a thousand poems, and in each poem a non-tenured faculty member barfed on about Marx and the inadequate way in which the semi-colon borders two independent clauses. The conversation turned to the alchemy of state imagery: in the background, the dangling corpse of the poet laureate hung from the vines of the cool and shady courtyard.

I stopped writing for a few years to examine the question of why I should write in the first place. I wanted desperately to write a poem which ended with a series of profitable suicides. I wanted to be the kind of man who took the culture to task for not engaging with sheep dung. Because my imagination had failed, I did not foresee my car driving full speed into a brick wall. I checked into a house of mercy and spent time with Thomas Merton. At night I hung poems from each orifice of the dangling corpse of the poet I wished to become.

In my free time, which became more or less indistinguishable from my overpriced time, I took long walks and began to notice the skulls, arms, legs, eyes, noses, and ears all around me. I did my best to arrange these body parts so that people from all walks of life would find poetry as they hiked through my alleyway. Vowing to never talk to anyone with a blog, I spent time with my dead grandmother. She warned me about the poet who was flung from an airplane for writing the wrong kind of verse. When he awoke he was Funes the Memorious and I was an expatriate in a nameless country in a featureless part of the world. Life was more or less uneventful until the dangling corpse began to recite the first of the *Duino Elegies* (translated by William Gass). Later, the dangling corpse transformed into scarecrows that hung in parallel rows across the cornfields of Kansas, Nebraska, and Missouri.

I was tired of practice. I wanted theory. So I thought about, but did not act upon, ways I could go beyond social critique and offer an alternative entry into the present tense, whose gates were blocked by poets who thought terrorism and lyricism were interchangeable. I gave up on the first person. Oscillating between plagiarism and parody, I began too many sentences with conjunctions. Eventually I returned to the last scene of Flaubert's "The Legend of St. Julian Hospitator." My lover was a leper and the war dead were ahistorical inventions apropos of an embedded unconscious that confused the word "poet" with "bureaucrat." Suddenly I was old, and I had no one to fucking talk to.

THE BOOK OF PRAYERS

To Whom It May Concern: Let us annihilate our bodies, says the first body in the Book of Prayers. Standing in a corner that is drawn onto a page of the Book, the body looks down at the other books and prays that the other bodies will die as the pages turn. The next page contains a body inside of a television screen. Veiled with hair, wrinkles, filth, and slobber, the body prays that the first blow it receives will be the last. Let my suffering end as it begins, the body says, and the screen shifts to an image of the body's skin. The camera climbs up a pole where the nation's flag is laminated in the skin of those who live on the pages and in the screens and in the dead valleys and ghost towns that dot the remains of the land. And let us pray for the nameless corpses, says the body on the cover of the Book of Prayers. The corpses are everyone and they are alone and alive in the grass and the sand and the forests and in our nostalgia for graves and tombstones and flowers that mark the memory of those bodies that once had names. And let us pray for the nameless corpses but let us not name them, says a body on a page of mutilated trees. The body looks out at a page of crawling and fluttering bodies that gyrate in the dead bushes of the dead fields near the books that mark those who have lost their names. A strange race of flies fills the page. They swarm and gurgle and suck the life out of everything and they live on the nameless bodies and they are the subject of the prayer uttered by a body on a page of fly-infested bodies. When the flies suck our blood, says the prayer, when the flies suck off our skin and blood and when our bones and hair fall out, let our bones and hair form towers up which our bodies will climb out of this book and into the Book of Eternal Ice. And the bodies ask the readers to pray with them. And the bodies tell the readers that by simply turning the pages they will be uttering the prayers for the dead. And the pages turn and there are bodies and murmurs emanate from them and we hear the prayer for those who died of hunger, for those who rotted away, for those who were eaten by dogs and vultures, for those whose faces were obliterated, for those whose eyes were removed from their skulls, for those who see and for those who refuse to see. For those who fell out of airplanes and for those who were thrown into the sea. For those who were buried in the desert and for those whose disembodied legs floated down rivers and were found by children playing on the muddy banks. And the pages flip and there are bodies praying atop barbed-wire fences for the years to pass quickly, for the forests to belch up the nameless bodies, for the elevation of the bodies stuck in mud, for the journeys to be short, for the prayers to be silent, for the faces to have names, for the eyes to be blank, for the mouths to have teeth, for the teeth to chew, for the food to give warmth, for the warmth to give blood, for the blood to give life, for the life to give more life—to the people and the grass and the air that are dead.

THE RELEVANCE OF POETRY
IN OUR CURRENT CLIMATE

He wanted to know how poetry could reclaim its place in every day life, and I thought of supervillains and tears and lava and floods and chains and Gods in the form of animals who rape and devour and I wondered how my imaginary world could explode his imaginary world and fill the imaginary worlds of readers with panic and stray dogs and poverty and whips and hospitals with defenestrated poets on the sidewalk and poets with missing limbs in each bed and on the wall in blood the verses of poets and poets fainting and screaming and giving birth from their mouths to other poets who do not need to be taught about the relevance of poetry in our current climate.

She said, "it" "really" "bothers" "me" "the" "way" "you" "use" "quotation" "marks." "So" "liberal" "you" "are" "with" "the" "quotation" "mark." "It's" "as" "if" "every" "word" "I" "say" "you" "want" "to" "put" "in" "quotation" "marks."

Revolution: Don't need to see it.
Power to the People: Don't need to hear it.
Das Kapital: Don't need to read it.

The poet was hired to teach poetry to children but the children left his courses thinking that poetry was something to slice people open with and when they heard iambic pentameter they fled into corners and howled. They knew poetry as a saw with which to remove the limbs of other poets and a cycle of sonnets was nothing more than blood collected from the dripping stump of a fool who hides in the world of language.

"Yes" "we" "already" "know" "all" "these" "things" "about" "poetry" "and" "more." "But" "please" "let" "us" "know" "how" "we" "can" "maintain" "a" "public" "dialogue" "about" "poetry."

Paste this poem with hot tar onto the naked skin of those who don't pay taxes, of those who are threats to the community, of those who use unregistered weapons, of those who snort cocaine, of those who don't vote, of those who succeed in the imagination, of those who fail in the imagination, of those who say no, no, no, instead of yes, yes, yes. Repeat as necessary until the subject confesses that he has never understood poetry in the first place, that he is a philistine with Ding-Dongs for ears and the chops of a hamster on sedatives.

The parents were upset because the poet had the tendency to keep the children after class to torment them with the insidious vapors of his verse. When the children came home after an afternoon of poetry, they had wet knickers, bruises, and weepy eyes; they complained of animals who were mistakes in the mind of God and which wanted to chew off their own tongues and buttocks.

To say that poetry has no political use is to deny the efficacy of poems doused in gasoline and shoved into the mouths of detainees and books of poetry lit on fire and placed into the pants of detainees who sincerely understand the fragility of identity which can be popped with the prick of a pin.

This poem is clunky and means just about nothing. This poem will be published in a book that will feature a painting by Paul Klee on the cover. This poem wishes it had a larger vocabulary. This poem is a passive member of the poetic community. Like all followers of the status quo, this poem looks to other poems for past precedent. This poem is not capable of deception or transcendence. Additionally, this poem is perfect for the occasion of being strapped against your will to a fence or gurney, electrocuted, or for having your face shoved in excrement. This is a contemporary poem. This poem allows you to be young, and to shake and move with the times.

THE BOOK OF VOICES

The Book of Voices begins where the Book of Prayer ends. The voices emanate from the mud which the bodies have turned into. The bodies that have turned into mud speak all at the same time but not in unison. Body ABC speaks of the last blow; body DEF speaks of the first blow; body GHI speaks of the blows he was forced to give to body JKL; and body JKL speaks of the moment of silence between blows, the moment of anticipation, relief, anxiety, fear, horror, and ecstasy that comes in the pauses between blows. Body MNO speaks of the clouds and the breeze that she fell through; body PQR speaks of how soft and wet the mud is; body STU speaks of the daggers, the blades, and all the instruments they jammed into the bottom of his toes; body VWX speaks of the bottom of the sea, the fish and the algae and all the dead animals she saw as she sunk deeper and deeper into the dead water. Body YZ speaks of the dogs that ate his leg. The bodies speak all at once, and to hear them is to listen to an opera of voices that are muffled by mud. They speak of their loves, true, but the loves they speak of are now chained to rocks, tied to animals, electrocuted, or buried in different puddles of mud. The priests who could save the bodies from this purgatory have lost all interest in God. The priests gather dead flowers and throw them on the graves of those who have names and in so doing they try to recall those who lost their names. The priests scribble in their books that solitude is now their god, and that the dead rivers and mountains and forests and deserts will come back to life when everyone here is alone. The priests pray to the flashes of electricity they see when the skin of the bodies is singed. The priests pray to the traces of gun powder that are left on the hands of the men ordered to obliterate the other men. The priests do not eat. Hunger is their god and in their hunger they pray for all those creatures for whom the church does not allow them to pray. The priests pray as if they are in foreign countries whose languages they cannot speak. The priests think there must be some relationship between their prayers and the secrets of the world, but they are wrong. There is no relationship between their prayers and anything living or dead. Their prayers benefit no one: not the ones who pray and not the ones who are prayed for; not the silence and not the voices. The prayers flee reality just as the voices flee reality. The prayers speak of light and water and death but no one is there to hear them. The voices of the bodies meld into the prayers and together they gather as shapeless formations on the horizon and they are like countries with no continent, like continents with no world, like worlds with no universe. The reader finds these formations in the Books; she finds them in the air between pages and in the spaces between punctuation marks and letters. The reader hears the prayers as she reads and in the prayers she hears an absence of breath, an absence of death, an absence of reason. The reader hears the prayers and in them she hears all that her body has tried not to be. One doesn't get used to this with time.

SMALL WOMAN, BIG MAN

Not to be devoured is the most perfect feeling

– CLARICE LISPECTOR
(translated by Elizabeth Bishop)

She scratched herself where no one scratches, and was deported for illegally crossing the border to make contact with the even more miniscule woman who lived in the village beyond. Arrested in her 12-inch home, she thanked the authorities for not stepping on her. Placed in a jar with air holes, she awaited her trial in a state of religious bliss.

He scratched his anus in the aisle of an airplane, and was held in solitary confinement in a third world country that did not acknowledge international law. Deprived of greasy hamburgers and Cheez Whiz, he flopped fish-like in his cell until the floor cracked beneath his weight. A prison guard filmed this new dance and sent it around the internet; and within a few days the enormous man unwittingly reached a notable level of cyber-fame. With time he lost enough weight to reach over his belly and comfortably wag his penis. This too was taped by the guards, but out of respect for moral values, the film was kept from the public.

THE BOOK OF NON-WRITING

There should be a writing of non-writing. Someday it will come.
A brief writing, without grammar, a writing of words alone.
Words without supporting grammar. Lost. Written, there.
And immediately left behind.

– MARGUERITE DURAS
(translated by Mark Pollizzotti)

It came. Words smashed out of the sky and from the mouths and off the pages and from the flesh and blood of the bodies and the words hit the readers and were destroyed like more bodies and the fields of the nation were littered with bodies and dead. Carcass love, they called it. Carcass economy, they called it. And the readers found the carcasses strewn across the pages and the readers came and stripped their innards and twirled intestines above their heads like lassos. The carcasses fell onto the pages and were taken away in wagons and trucks and they were replaced with new carcasses that were sold for words before the flies laid eggs and the wounds had time to fester. FALSE CARCASS ECONOMY! Will the souls of the carcasses miss themselves when they die? Will the bodies whose lips slurp out the souls of the carcasses miss themselves when they die? Will the words from the bodies who slurp out the souls of the carcasses cease to exist when the bodies themselves die? The readers grovel in the pages and find themselves in ditches with the carcasses but they do not know the rules of the false carcass economy. In this book the readers can feel their feet being removed.

In this book the readers can feel the splash of abattoir blood that sprinkles the page with poems. How do you know if the poems have too many bubbles? That is, how do you know if the blood of the poems has too many bubbles? When we speak of our own lives, says the collective voice of the readers, we certainly don't mean human life. On the page the readers find themselves crawling around like quadrupeds with hands full of grass and earth uprooting plants and trees setting out for home and not getting far counting corpses on the fields to hell with animals there is God grinding his teeth with joy forging his way through the ruins of failing flesh there is the machine that has annihilated the bulk of humanity is it semen or is it a carburetor that makes us unrecognizable we know who we are through decay and in someone else's story this is a lot worse than knocking your own brains out with good results then drinking tea with sugar and milk and suddenly feeling revived then exploding with words and speaking with animals and sinking in mud and being found by peasants who clean turds and who are like silent gods with holes in their shoes it is horrible to eat horrible to bulge in the belly with food horrible to blink when so many can't blink oh to ruminate once more on the air polluted with liability on the hair singed from pollution the eyes burning fingers shrivelling the exact moment of ending will not come for many millennia we will not be able to document it it will document us it's okay to kill some bodies speak of nothing and you're lucky to make friends flank kidney liver swollen body on the sand who are you now that I am speaking with a mouth full of words that do not belong to me I crawl across the page and I don't know if I'm dying or dead.

THE SYNCHRONOUS ASPECT
OF THE BITTER FOLLY

The teenagers smear blood on the torsos of dogs and children.

And the rotting stillness is stalked by the angels of the white people at 7-Eleven.

And the telephone calls to the "shepherds in their yellow corn" are placed via gunshot to the skull.

A villager dies and her cousin buys a lottery ticket at the local bodega.

He scratches and snarls and places a bomb in the garbage can in the alley.

Post-detonation all the garbage cans are removed to protect us from villagers and cousins.

And we fear ourselves as we fear giant T-bone steaks from England.

And we fear the towers of trash on our streets.

And we fear out of convenience and we fear out of tenderness.

And we fear out of love and we fear out of innocence.

And we connect to the world by shining our headlights at the men who sit in their cars and masturbate to the image of darkness.

And the boys who can't imagine a different world, car jack just for the fun of it.

And as the illegal immigrants struggle to explain their illnesses, the sentences collapse under the weight of their syntax:

And the colored girls go:

I! have! pulmonary! congestion!

I! have! cholera!

I! have! phlebitis!

THE BOOK OF WAITING

The book waits. The readers wait, for the bodies to find the bones in the muddy solitude. The bodies rest one atop the other. Shelter for the one on bottom. Guilt for the one on top. The mud swells up around them, and the reader digs through it, thinking, what will I do as I wait to become a body drowning in mud? The question is about rhythm. That is, the question is about how many breaths will be taken, and with what regularity. Through reading the reader becomes physically unrecognizable to herself. But what of the flesh attached to the electrical current: does it love the skin the way skin loves blood? The reader reads this book under a sunset on the last day of summer. The sun is a candy pink ball low over the dead city where the cats rub wildly against each other to make sure they are alive. This is a land where bodies in mud are indigenous, and disembodied arms and legs are native to the forests and rivers, and yet the pages of this book are completely deserted. It's not that they are blank. They are beyond blank. It's a book that doesn't have pages. And yet the readers wait because the image on the cover leads them to believe that the pages may soon appear, and that on those pages there will be words, and that the words will be dead, but new words will fall out of them. And in those words there will be a toddler just learning to speak. And he will see all the books in a flame. And he will point to the flame and say hot hot hot. And all the voices will say with him hot hot hot. And the book that is empty even of pages will be a safe zone for the bodies fleeing the barracks where hundreds of nights end in unison and where the words are rotten assets and the bodies are rotten assets in the false carcass economy where there is no one to identify the world as world. Forgive the pages for wanting to feel important as they hide from their book. The pages laugh as they flee the readers who puncture themselves when they trip on the glass-dotted bodies in the mud. Stitch up the chin of the reader for he has fallen on a destroyed face which talks to the sea as if it were an umbrella that politely shelters the dead grass. Full stop. Period. A reader murmurs through her belly that the pages are lost in the fog storm that has swallowed the valley and the fog storm sits between the covers of the books which is what happens to a country when it dies. Full stop. Period. The assets rot and the words rot and the pages rot and this goes on until the citizens stop their panic and the infrastructure of solitude crumbles and the private bodies are no longer private their decay is public and the readers wait for the pages to appear and for the book to be written so they can live once more a life where decay and maturity are identical experiences. To live in books is like this. Every syllable obliterates every other syllable and the reader is alone with a book that does not yet exist and as she reads she thinks it will be the only witness to her sinking into the mud and she hopes the sentences will not black out and she hopes the page will not be barbed-wire again rather she hopes the book will be more like a quick drink of poison. Her face is like a country now. It is ready to fall off onto the pages that will fall into the book that will fall into the hands of the citizens as they fall into the flames, singing: this is water, water, water.

CRAZY JANE FINDS A DOG

At night I hunt explosions and in the day I invest my liquidity into the alchemy of trash and sewage.

To not be devoured, to not be devoured, to not be devoured:

I hide with the white bitch in the mud, praying to not be devoured.

In the cemetery, I lurk in the silence of the men who wear the shirts I fold so neatly: I eat them with my eyes; I spit them from my armpits.

I rub their skulls with the bottom of my fungal foot:

I read them like a crane, like a bulldozer, like an abattoir.

I read them like voltage up the leg of a monkey, like voltage up the leg of a whore who is the only man who can remember every single angle from which the piss came out of the cat, like leeches on the back of a whore who is the only man who can remember every single drip, and the moment before the drip, and the furiously pissing cat, and the cat in profile, sprinkling the land with poetry.

My ugly toes on the moss, the stupidity of my ankles: here, looking onto this land of piss, I exalt my own lethargy.

Here, in the mud, every thought I think is a word between fear and love, every thought I think is a whore with so many choices that all he can do is slash his wrists and refuse to die.

I do not bother anyone, and no one asks me questions.

Now that I take care of the white bitch, I have gained the respect of my family.

THE BOOK OF DECOMPOSITION

*It is in the tranquillity of decomposition that I remember
the long confused emotion which was my life.*

– SAMUEL BECKETT

Here the reader rots alongside of the book and its characters. A man in the
opening chapter pulls strands of hair off his head; the reader does the same.
A man feels maggots crawling all over his skin; the reader feels the same.
The book begins in a butcher shop that has been looted by poor bodies
that tear out cow intestines and unravel them in the dead grass behind the
butcher's shed. The bodies see books in the intestines whose characters are
their mirror images, and the bodies grow terrified of themselves. They run
into the woods but they hate nature so they take shelter in the stables where
rotten bodies hide in the hay. The dead bodies in this stable are countries
and the protagonist says USA USA your assets are rotten you are dying and
Haiti your huts have flooded and your citizens kill for bread and beans and
New Orleans your bodies float in puddles of shit hey China your babies are
drinking poisoned milk and Mexico your peasants cannot hear or see and in
the USA the assets are rotten the Bolivians sell less coke on Wall Street the
Iranians don't have enough money to blow Israel off the map the Russians
can't build new weapons to sell to the Syrians and Venezuelans the Cuban
doctors and prostitutes service bodies that live far away the nations conduct
business in body parts here are the legs of our citizens we will trade you
for arms and kidneys and here take these eyes and livers and give us hearts

and tongues and intestines. Full stop. Period. In the end it's unclear if it's the reader or the characters who request some form of movement to free the bodies from the sorcery of global capital. Nevertheless, the request is granted and the book ends happily with the entrance of a saint who has so much love that he heals the sores of the bodies with his tongue and prepares them once more to succeed as cosmopolitan bodies in a ring of fantastically interconnected commerce. The book ends with a giant ejaculation behind the butcher shop where the bodies rub against each other as if there were no barriers to keep them from consummating their fiscal intimacies. And in the final scene water streams off the pages, cleansing the skin of the readers in a climax of diluvial bubbling.

BUREAUCRATIC LOVE PREVENTION GAME

Two bodies intertwine on the edge of a great ravine gazing lustfully at the dead flowers and wondering what will happen to their bodies if they cannot attach themselves to other bodies. In the village the bodies are electrocuted for coming into contact with other bodies. The bureaucrats hypothesize that the bodies will adapt and learn to live with the jolts of electricity that run through their blood and bones when they touch other bodies. The bodies soon adapt and find the smell of singed skin to be aphrodisiacal. The bodies observe each other as they negotiate the currents of electricity that ignite with each touch. I love you more and more as your body shrivels to ash, says one body to another. In the lookout towers the bureaucrats record the moment with pride--in their ability to determine future behavior. The air is encoded so that the bodies will only touch if they think that there is a hole in the sky into which they will fall at the moment when their love can not be detained. The bodies flash in the night and the words that emerge from their mouths evaporate as soon as they are spoken. The bodies push through the electric jolts and commune beyond the bureaucrats' wildest expectations. But when the electricity ends the bodies retreat from each other and do not speak until another body in the village is jolted. The expressions on the bodies' faces are impossible to describe when they try to sneak in affectionate words amid the jolts of electricity that hit them. Lasting image 2493-132 shows a body being struck down by lightning as another body attempts to pull it into the swampy mud. Lasting image 342.229a2 shows a village full of motionless bodies sprawled on the ground as if dead. The bureaucrats do not anticipate the complete lethargy that overtakes the bodies when they are not struck with jolts. In the face of this lethargy, the bureaucrats are afraid of the silence, the stillness, the darkness, and the determination of the bodies to move only for the sake of attaching themselves to other bodies, only for the sake of being jolted by electricity. The silence in the daytime is impossible. Thus the bureaucrats, in order to counteract this lethargy, enforce a culture of non-stop diurnal movement: from sunrise to sunset the bodies walk in circles all day without touching each other. No body can be silent or sedentary while the sun is out. In the daylight the bodies circle endlessly while at night they wait for the love they will receive. The electricity on the body is nourishing. The flashes in the night are nourishing.

THE BOOK OF COLLAPSING NATIONS

This book begins with an image of a man in an expensive suit ripping out his hair and setting himself on fire as a nation of toddlers gathers around him screaming hot hot hot. It's a comedy, this book, and thus the cranes that come to remove the citizens from their beds are decorated with birds and flowers. The men who drive the cranes are happy; on some pages they are naked and when they hit the switch the orchestra breaks into a Beethoven symphony as the mechanical arm of the pretty machine reaches through a window or a chimney, plucks out the citizens and drops them on the street where they are ushered to a bridge over the river. I'd give my right arm to stay in my bed, says one man, and sure enough his right arm is sliced off and tossed into the river. I'd bend over backwards to make sure my baby can stay in her crib, says a mother, and with those words her back is broken and she is tossed into the river to float with the other bodies that traffic in the magic of capital. The next chapter begins with an army of toddlers shouting God bless the bulldozer God bless the bulldozer, and with this entry the bulldozer moves earth and rubble out of the way, and out from the ground jump bearded men in white robes who clutch shit-smeared holy books and break into song. Their bodies have been destroyed; blood flows from open wounds and on the ground around them we see the arms and legs that the militia will toss into the river as soon as the song of the bearded men ends. The bearded men sing songs that the people love: anthems and show tunes and though they have been brutalized underground for months they are happy to be alive as they dance on one leg through the city. Meanwhile, across town, in the next chapters, the militias board up the shop windows while citizens hoist television screens on their backs, groaning and searching for someone to buy what never belonged to them in the first place. And hey look there's another man in an expensive suit; he boards up the windows of his penthouse, opens a holy book, rests it under his head, and puts a bullet through his brain. The collapsing city is not like a cloud of dust, rather it's an electrical outlet that suddenly loses power in the middle of an ordinary night. The reader comes to a market but there are no oranges or fish or chicken or beans or bread or coffee or lemons or anything else to stave off hunger. The nation is humid and smelly; trash piles up in towers on street corners and the toddlers dig through the towers looking for apples and adults and flowers; and the statues of the nation's heroes have been beheaded and briefcase-clutching entrepreneurs fall out of windows and water is dozens of dollars a gallon and the bodies that fall out of the sky are not honored when they drop instead the scavengers search their clothes and find the keys to their houses that have already been taken over by other scavengers. It's impossible to read this book without laughing—at the dead houses and dead churches and dead streets wherein the scavengers dig fearfully for some verification that the nation will continue to collapse for at least another few years.

NEIGHBORHOOD POEM

When the SRO finally opened after much protest from the block council the neighborhood was filled with mentally ill citizens who had been thrown out of psychiatric hospitals in the Reagan years.

And the warehouse at the corner was demolished to make room for a building with $400,000 condos.

And the condos went up next to the public housing unit which was kept in the neighborhood to assure a mix of incomes.

And when the youth congregated in front of the public housing unit, the police drove by slowly, which prevented the youth from smoking marijuana and mugging passersby and residents of the condos.

And when a youth was shot on the sidewalk between the condo unit and the public housing unit, police tape went up on the sidewalk in front of both buildings, physically connecting the residents in a way their shared geography could not.

And the overpriced health food shop, in response to repeated requests from confused residents of the SRO, put up a sign in their window informing customers that food stamps were not accepted.

And a new condo unit was constructed across the street from the public housing unit.

And within a month all six apartments sold for $390,000 a piece.

And the space that was formerly occupied by the hair dresser whose business had been a front for a meth-dealer was re-opened by a spa that catered only to men, and which charged $80/hour for a massage, and $150 for a massage, hair cut, and pedicure.

And the owner of the diner that opened in 1948 resisted closure, but could no longer afford his lease.

And the foodies cheered as the cupcake shop opened next to the overpriced market that sells nothing but olive oil and imported cheese and chorizo.

And the gluten-free bakery opened next to the shop that sells fancy chocolates with ginger and cardamom that opened in the space formerly occupied by the shop that sold fancy shirts for men that opened in the space formerly occupied by a shop that sold expensive baby clothes that opened in the space formerly occupied by the family-run hardware store that had been in the neighborhood for thirty-two years.

And when the city rebuilt the metro station, the construction forced the dry cleaner and the bagel shop out of business.

And after the construction was complete, a Panera Bakery and another overpriced health food store opened in place of the dry cleaner and the bagel shop.

And the Sicilian bakery opened in the space that was formerly occupied by the coffee shop whose name I no longer remember despite the fact that it had been in the neighborhood for so many years.

And the owner of the gym suddenly closed without prior warning. He locked the doors and fired all of his employees, including the illegal immigrants who swept the floors and cleaned the semen off the walls of the sauna.

And the members of the gym roamed the streets like refugees in track suits, looking for tread mills and hand jobs.

And Angel's Restaurant went out of business for reasons that were never made clear to their customers.

And the lesbian gourmands took foie gras off the menu and replaced it with a vegetarian Wellington.

And the bank knew what I was going to say before I even asked how to protect my credit card from the owner of the gym who rumor had it tried to commit suicide after suddenly closing his business.

And from the rumor mill we learned that the guy who owned the gym, Mr. Gay Chicago-1987, actually owned a Cheetah; he did not, however, adopt two kids from South Africa, although one person on the rumor mill claimed to have seen him with his two adopted South African kids at Mommy and Me Yoga the day after he closed the business, the day after he debited the accounts of all 10,000 members of his three area gyms, two days before he tried to kill himself.

And the guy at the dry cleaner lost me as a customer after he refused to refund my shirt that he ruined by staining the arm pits with bleach. He refused to refund my shirt because he was fearful that admitting guilt would harm his reputation.

And the video camera above his door kept me and other disappointed customers from smashing the windows of his shop after hours.

And the video camera kept junkies from buying drugs in front of the dumpster.

And the downstairs neighbor drove his car through the garage and blamed it on a faulty accelerator.

THE BOOK OF EQUALITY

Here the readers gather to watch the books die. They die suddenly, as if thrown from an airplane, or from spontaneous cardiac arrest. They live, and then suddenly they die, and the reader who watches this is at the moment of the books' death bombarded with images documented through the smiling lipstick face of a journalist who has shown up to report on the death of the books. The milk was poisoned and forty-two babies died, she laughs, as she fondles the ashes of the dead books. And the death of forty-two babies is equal in value to the death of this book which is equal in value to the ninety-year old woman who shot herself while the sheriff waited at her door with an eviction notice which is equal in value to the collapsing of the global economy which is equal to the military in country XYZ seizing the land of the semi-nomadic hunters and cultivators of crops who have lived in the local rain forest for thousands of years. The reader opens a dead book and finds an infinite amount of burnt ash between the bindings, and when the ash blows in the wind the lipstick says that every death in the world is equal to every other death in the world which is equal to every birth in the world which is equal to every act of dismemberment which is equal to the death of a jungle which is equal to the collapse of the global economy; and hey look there's another lady falling out of a window; she looks about equal to the poet hurled out of his country for words he wrote but which did not belong to him and whose death is about equal to the girl who was shot on the bus on her way to school this morning which is just about the same as the bearded man whose head was shoved into a sac while water was dumped over it and he died for an instant and came back to life and talked and talked and that's about equal to the steroid illegally injected into the arm of a beautiful man who makes forty million dollars a year for injecting his arms with steroids so he can more skillfully wave a wooden stick at a ball, and in the ash we see the truest democracy there ever was: hey look it's a little baby found in a dumpster how equal you are says the smiling lipstick to the civilized nation whose citizens walk the flooded streets looking for their homes, and in the ashes of the dead book the dead streets are equal to the eating disorders of movie stars which are equal to the dead soldiers who are equal to the homeruns which are equal to the bomb dropped by country ABC over weddings in the village of country XYZ which is equal to the earth swallowing up and devouring all of its foreigners which is just about equal to the decline in literacy in the most educated nation in the planet. There is no end to this book. There are no paragraph breaks to interrupt the smiling lipstick that goes on and on in one string of ashy words about how the declaration of peace is equal to the resumption of war and how the bodies that fall are equal to the birds that ascend and how the bomb in the Eiffel Tower is equal to the rising cost of natural gas, and the murmurs of the voices in the mud are equal to the murmurs of the expensive suits falling out of buildings and these are equal to the silence that kills with one breath and coddles life with another.

DREAM OF LAUGHTER AND SILENCE

The extreme affliction which overtakes human beings
does not create human misery, it merely reveals it.

– SIMONE WEIL
(translated by Arthur Wills)

If time were an animal, it would be a sheep, said the barbaric writer to the sheep as he climbed inside its fleece. The barbaric writer, a miniscule poet in a world of miniscule poets, snapped his fingers, and populated the hair of the sheep with thousands of barbaric writers. He climbed atop the sheep's horn as the sheep and its cargo of barbaric writers marched to the center of town.

This is a story about laughter, but it has its roots in a story which has nothing to do with laughter.

There once was a village where everyone died of laughter. I read about it in a novel, but the novel was so boring that I stole the village and put it into my childhood. The village is now in the backyard of the house I grew up in. There is a school, a synagogue, a bakery, a post office, a library, a diner, and a hospital, and when you enter each building the people greet you not with words, and not with silence, and not with handshakes, smiles, or any other gestures, rather they greet with you laughter: terrifying, barbaric laughter.

One day the barbaric writer brought a sheep into the village. He stuck a bomb in the sheep's fleece. And when he led the sheep into the synagogue, the bomb detonated: a mesmerizing explosion of laughter. The oil from the Sabbath candles dripped off the bima and formed a river of laughter, a waxy river of laughter in which the miniscule barbaric writers floated and swam like happy little children.

If time were an animal, my father used to laugh, as he sat on the balcony of the house I grew up in, it would be a sheep who would stay at the back of the flock as it fled from the wolves and poets who devoured its brothers. And his most hideous laughter rocked the entire village.

Civilization, wrote Freud, has to use its utmost efforts in order to set limits to man's aggressive instincts and to hold them in check by physical reaction-formations. But what could hold in check the horrible, beautiful, mundane, hypnotic laughter that filled every molecule of our village?

This is the first line of one of the most famous verses from one of our most famous poets, who happens to be my father:

Haaaaaaaaaaaaaaaaaaaaa. aHa! Ha Ha Haaaaaaaaa. Ahahahahaho.

Which means something along the lines of: Silence is a cliché which never gets old.

One night, when I was a child, I listened to my father tell his tale of exile. He was forced out of the village of silence and into the village of laughter when a policeman and a squad of silent bureaucrats came into his home, stuck a knife to his throat, and ordered him to speak. He spoke, so as to prevent the blade from slicing his neck, but he knew he was violating the sacred decrees of his village. And so for each word he spoke, he was required to march an equivalent number of kilometers. That day he spoke 212 words, and was thus forced to walk 212 kilometers, and from there he had to walk another 2 kilometers to the closest village, the village of laughter, where he was to live the rest of his life.

This is a story of snorts, chuckles, hoots, and guffaws.

Snakes squirm out of my father's mouth when he laughs: their hiss, a hiss of mirth, a hiss of dread, a hiss of laughable sorrow.

Why did they force you out of the silent village, I asked my father with my trademark monotonous giggle.

I was forced to flee the silent village, chuckled my father, because they knew I would never speak.

If time were an animal, said the barbaric writer to the sheep, as he climbed inside its fleece, it would be a sheep. My father laughed these words with optimism, though in reality he knew that time was nothing more than a wolf in wolf's clothing.

One day, my father, in an act of uncontrollable nostalgia, fled the village of laughter and walked the 214 kilometers back to his native village, the village of silence, but instead of finding the lost land of his childhood, he found nothing more than an empty space, emptied of absolutely everything, and thus he tried, desperately, to fill the void with time.

There was no longer silence in the village of silence, but there was not sound either, which is to say that the silence of my father's childhood was the silence of not-speaking, while the silence of the present was the silent betrayal of history.

My father laughed. He laughed the loudest, longest laugh that could possibly come out of his throat, and I swear, I saw this: the bones of the dead residents of the village of silence fell out of his laughter; they fell out of his mouth, then levitated, and twisted into a giant bird, an eagle which took off into flight, and gracefully drifted through the clouds, describing wide and perfect arcs above my father's head.

Quit laughing, the eagle squawked at my father. Quit your infernal laughter.

But my father could not stop laughing, though he knew with certainty that life was the opposite of humor.

Quit laughing, the eagle squawked again, and when my father did not stop laughing, the eagle, to punish him, spat a mouthful of seeds a few feet from where my father stood. The seeds sunk into the earth, germinated, and soon sprouted into a skyscraper. No, the eagle did not fly into the building, and blow it up, though it very well could have. Instead, the eagle turned the building into a military compound occupied by miniature barbaric poets, and their dogs, to whom the poets strapped bombs and sent them off to the nearest urban centers, where day after day the dogs exploded in the streets, in schools, in office buildings, hospitals, and shopping malls.

My father stood outside this building for many years, laughing, and as the years passed I slowly turned into him: a frozen man with no other talent than the talent for infinite laughter.

One day, however, something changed. I was standing outside the building, laughing as usual, when a boy approached and began to laugh, a laugh which was exactly the same as my laugh, and I instantly understood, the way you understand things in dreams, that this boy was my father, and that my father was also me. And so the boy laughed, and because he laughed I no longer had to laugh; I was unfrozen, and now, for the first time in years, I was finally able to be silent.

I began to walk.

I walked for several months, until one day, I entered an office building in downtown Chicago, stepped into the elevator, and got off on the seventeenth flood, where I met for the first time my wife, a practitioner of silence, in an office where speech and laughter were forbidden. I took her by the hand, and we began to walk: we left the office, descended the stairs, and headed northwest to a part of town which was suprisingly leafy. Finally, we reached an auditorium, where hundreds of silent young people marched in perfect circles outside the front door.

I said to my wife: "This is my favorite place."

But the seconds the words left my mouth, I knew I had done something terribly wrong. For suddenly there was commotion, and we found ourselves, along with the silent marchers, being ushered by an invisible force into the auditorium.

We stood still in the lobby, and we could see that on the other side of the doors, in the theatre, the marchers were now on their knees with their arms tied behind their backs, their faces draped with hoods. A moment later a muscular young man ordered us to freeze. He had a shaved head, and when he wiggled the index finger on his right hand I understood that the people on the other side of the door, in the theatre, were being executed, via silent gunshot, and all because I had said that this was my favorite place.

I was disgusted with myself, not because I had sentenced the marchers to die, but because I recognized how desperately I wished to control something.

I ran out of the building, and now I was alone, on the streets of an empty city whose residents were locked away under a perpetual curfew of darkness, a darkness so deep that I walked over to the edge of the city and fell into a new city where I would never be able to sleep.

THE BOOK OF RUBBLE

To begin there is the history of roads. Grass, mud, dirt, pavement, potholes, sidewalks, white lines, fire hydrants, bricks, manholes, sewers, bulldozers, cement trucks, etc... The empire could not have been built had the roads not hidden the corpses of those who built them. An interlude: an author one day came to write the history of the roads, and he was told that they were in the Books, but when he went to the tower of books he could not locate the Book of Roads, and after searching for many weeks he finally found a footnote in another book, the Book of Silent Collapse, which indicated that the Book of Roads was nothing more than a minor character in a larger book, the Book of Rubble, which the author was able to locate and translate for the readers, who sat in puddles of mud waiting for some sign that one day they would learn their own names, and that one day those names would be engraved on the slabs under which they would spend eternity. In this book, and in this country, it's not just arms and legs that fall out of windows. The men in expensive suits toss bags of paper from their windows and set them aflame, and as the bags of paper fall so fall the men; and as the paper and bodies splatter, a miniature market forms out of their detritus. The first to arrive at the market are the Association of Blind Citizens, who have been led to the scene by their dogs who smelled something funny on the horizon. Here, take this paper, and I'll give you some bones, says one blind citizen to another. The blind citizens whack each other over the head with the bones of the men in expensive suits. The paper flies everywhere, and the dogs tear them to shreds; and as the blind citizens pummel each other, the rubble murmurs in the distance: bulldozers, cranes, abattoirs, bodies in mud, sinfoniettas of white noise, gun shot, sirens.

And the architects murmur:

We love this building so much we will destroy it.

And the authors murmur:

We love our books so much we will destroy them.

And the fathers murmurs:

We love our families so much we will bury them in the mud with the other bodies, and we will stand above their slabs, and we will listen to their murmurs, and we will murmur as they murmur so that we do not have to hear the sounds of their infernal murmuring.

And the citizens murmur:

We love our country so much that we will make it a mound of rubble.

An expensive suit hurls a bag of paper from his window and sets it on fire, and as the paper crumbles, the houses of the citizens crumble; all through the nation citizens clutch their moldy timber, their moldy floorboards, their leaky roofs, their faulty chimneys, their shattered windows, their rotting bricks and siding in the hopes that they will salvage some memory of their lives from the wrecking balls that destroy their homes.

The homeless citizens now roam the streets like donkeys, carrying everything they own on their backs. They march to the bridges and throw themselves into the water with their belongings strapped to their bodies so that they will sink helplessly to the bottom of the river. Tables and chairs and sofas and desks and bookshelves and beds and television sets and lamps and coffee makers now float down the river with the disembodied arms and legs that are native to this part of the world.

ILLINOIS

I

The state swallowed you whole and spit you out and hacked you up

It was in the middle of the country and when we had been together we stood on the banks of rivers where the green sludge bubbled and where the fingers that accidentally touched water were taken to the laboratory to look inside the skin and on the surface of the skin and in the blood and pores and cells to see what happens when the impermanent touches the permanent in the middle of a state that's dead

I looked for you when the water expelled us

My love I looked for you in the alleyways and hospitals and brothels and when I spoke I found it impossible to use adjectives

This was the only way I found it bearable to speak of you

You didn't exist and I knew this

You had been spit out of the ground and I knew this

You had been spit up and shredded with the paper that no longer had value and I knew this

You had been shredded with the dollar bills and I knew this and I looked for you and when I came to your town I put up pictures with your name and a few words about you and I went to new towns where no one had ever loved you

I moved on

I didn't forget but I had decided that within the state there was another state that held you and within that state the guards who controlled the borders watched and I knew there was a state where the people governed themselves and you were there and I thought of you as I roamed the state looking not for you but for my own body and I knew you were in this state guarding the bodies saying prayers over the body parts worshiping the hair the arms the fingers the eyes of those spit up by other states you were the guardian of body parts and to see you this way gave me strength enough to walk through this state in a state that was drowning in nothing

11

Let me be more specific

I came to a bridge in a city

I wouldn't let go of your hand

You hadn't spoken since I lost you and when I put my ear to your ear I could hear your voice

You said I am not in the sky

You spoke directly

It's comforting to think you might have spoken in code but you did not know how to speak in code and neither do I

Let me be more specific

We were crossing a bridge over a river that was not in your city but that led to a river that ran through your city

It was suicide week and I thought of flinging myself off the bridge with the others

I thought for a moment I might find you if I flung myself off the bridge

The voice between your ears said jump jump don't jump don't jump now jump already

We stood on the bridge watching the bodies dance the dance of body parts swaying in the wind as they stood on the edge of the bridge

You told me a story

You said once there was a body that threw money into the river before jumping

And it was this that changed everything

It was the money the body threw into the river that finally kept the others from jumping

The bodies came to the bridge ready to throw themselves in

The bodies came to the bridge but when they saw the money flung into the river they decided that it was not suicide they wanted it was a world with no money

They convinced all of their neighbors to throw their money into the river

The citizens of the town threw all of their money into the river

They threw all of their credit cards into the river

They burned the banks

They burned their computers

They smashed the windows of anyone in the city whose life had anything to do with preserving the flow of capital

They banned the use of certain words: credit market, liquidity, etc...

The bodies stopped jumping and we found a home on the bridge

You told me this in your head and your voice was afraid of nothing

I I I

I stood on the bridge watching the water move away from itself

I came to find you my love you live here now

She is my love too and my love too said the voices of the straggling men with their fish

We're not from around here, they said

No one in this country sits on a bridge selling fish, they said

We're from a different time zone, they said

We're from the ship that refuses to return to these waters

We're from the Big Bang or at least the moment before the earth swelled up like an over-boiled egg

The man was slapped when he said these words

We don't use similes around here, a man said

He said forgive him he's from Wisconsin they have a virginal faith in language there

It's ridiculous to be from anywhere, a voice said

We are the men from purgatory, another voice said

The river was drying up before our eyes

It looked like a few drops of piss and for a moment I saw you there

I called out to tell you about this very second on this very spot on earth

I am on the bridge I said and you heard me and stepped out of the river

You filled your mouth with water and when you spat a cat came towards me

I knew it was you for when you spoke little bubbles formed on the river and they were poems to our evaporating bodies

You said the world presses in on us from every side

It scatters dust across our mouths and covers us with our blood

You said my mouth is filled with 270 caliber bullets and they taste like little orgasms

I jumped towards you and your skin was quicksand and in that moment there was no water to absorb us

Then the Mississippi rumbled and the Missouri called for the heads of our Christian neighbors

The Missouri rumbled and the Ohio called for the heads of anyone who had ever touched you

You said I believe in the river because it will be here when I die but it was disappearing as you spoke

I said I believe in the bridge because it will be here my love when you and the earth disappear

I V

The river had swallowed you and as you disappeared a triangle of birds flew over our heads

I saw the birds and thought of sky-written advertisements for a shampoo I'd used when I was a child but if only the birds were actually the secret police and if only the river was a torturer or a bed of electricity then at least I would have some excuse for not wanting to stand here anymore

I felt a woman's legs against my knees but they were not your legs and they were not my knees

The ground was murmuring the cuckoo talk of the thirsty soil

The river had swallowed you and as you disappeared a triangle of birds flew over our heads

The city sounds were like roosters and the men with their briefcases passed by spitting with their eyes and the air curved and the milk jumped and the moment I said goodbye to you I knew the forest was a vacuum and I knew the threads of light I saw on the other side of the trees were borders between the world as it is and the world as I wished it to be

There was nothing abnormal in this

It was perfectly normal and though no one talks about nature here I sensed that the grass was all there was even though it had been ripped from the streets many decades ago

I put a handful of bullets in my mouth with a spoon and wished I could swallow them the way your voice had been swallowed by the river but my body would not comply

My body was a voice atop another voice and when I pushed my finger into your grace it was just the grace of the floorboards creaking the ghosts of on and on

THE BOOK OF INTERFERING BODIES

I've noticed that writers who are superb at making love are much more rarely great writers than those who are scared and not so good at it.

–MARGUERITE DURAS
(translated by Barbara Bray)

The book begins with an epigraph: "every body that is not my body is a foreign country." The reader opens the book to find bodies with words all over them. And when the reader finds these bodies, the words make her feel fearful, as if she is speaking to a master bureaucrat, a police officer, or a doctor. The words project authority, but this is an illusion. The words do not have authority. It is the bodies, soaked in simple words, which make the reader feel inadequate. On the first page of the book a body wiggles in a grave, and words ascend out of his mouth and hair. There is an electrical current running through these words and from one page to another. On the second page, the words illuminate the paper, and out of the light appears a bureaucrat whose eyes are two television sets inside of which there are two writers trying to make love, but there is something on the TV screens that comes between them. It is the carcass of a dog, and then a man in an expensive suit who falls out of a window, and then a baby lifting her head out of the desert sand, then a disembodied arm, then a starving body sleeping on cold streets, then an African war, an Asian war, a European war, an American war, then radiation poisoning, polluted baby formula, children with missing limbs. And this goes on for pages. Each page is an image that prevents the bodies from making love. A strong wind starts to blow through the pages and a young girl appears with television sets for eyes. The wind makes the light turn neon and now in the two eyes that are television sets the readers sees her own body opening up like a volcano and flooding the pages with ash and lava and all the small animals that she inadvertently trapped as she went about the business of life. Two more young bodies with television sets for eyes appear inside the television in the eyes of the young girl, and in the blue screens the reader sees herself trying to make love to another reader, but their bodies are blocked by cities, highways, religious institutions, languages, doors, automobiles, curtains, valleys, frontiers, oceans, wars, scientific advancements, clocks, weapons, forests, darkness, collapsing nations, and light. A man comes into the television screens. He opens his mouth and a famine falls onto the pages. He is an emigrant, and through his eyes he communicates that he is homesick for his former body, for the wool rags he used to wrap himself in, for the hair they cropped before they threw him in the river, before they sunk him in the mud and made great economic advancements as he dropped to the bottom of the sea. I am not an individual, the man says, as he steps between the bodies who wish to make love. I am a dead mountain; my mouth is a bloody carcass; my belly is a dead river; my face is a city drowning in a storm. Perhaps I better go back to the valley, he says, but as he tries to step out of the television screen, he falls to the ground with a thud, and lays there like a pile of rocks.

ACKNOWLEDGEMENTS

Thanks to the editors of the following publications for publishing some of the poems in this book:

1913 a journal of forms; Action, Yes; Columbia Poetry Review; Copper Nickel; Denver Quarterly; Diode; La Petite Zine; Lamination Colony; Left Facing Bird; Mandorla: New Writing from the Americas; Milk Magazine; New Orleans Review; Ocho; P.F.S Post; Sawbuck; Seven Corners; SleepingFish; string of small machines; Transformation; and *Wheelhouse Magazine*

Some of these poems appeared in the chapbook *Failure in the Imagination* published by Bronze Skull Press. Others appeared in *One Size Fits All*, an e-chapbook published by Scantily Clad Press; and others were published in the anthology *Malditos Latinos Malditos Sudacas: Poesia Iberoamericana Made in USA* (El billar de Lucrecia, Mexico City).

ISBN: 978-0-9844598-2-7

Design and typesetting by HR Hegnauer
Cover art: Drawing of "The Dead Factory" by Laurie Lipton (www.laurielipton.com)
Type set in Garamond

Cataloging-in-publication data is available
From the Library of Congress

Distributed by University Press of New England
One Court Street
Lebanon, NH 03766
www.upne.com

Nightboat Books
Callicoon, New York
www.nightboat.org

NIGHTBOAT BOOKS

Nightboat Books, a nonprofit organization, seeks to develop audiences for writers whose work resists convention and transcends boundaries. We publish books rich with poignancy, intelligence, and risk. Please visit our website, www.nightboat.org, to learn about our titles and how you can support our future publications.

The following individuals have supported the publication of this book. We thank them for their generosity and commitment to the mission of Nightboat Books:

Kazim Ali
Jennifer Chapis
Sarah Heller
Elizabeth Motika
Laura Sejen
Benjamin Taylor

This book has been made possible, in part, by a grant from the New York State Council on the Arts Literature Program.

State of the Arts

NYSCA